MANAGEMENT Boll**ks

How to talk your way to the top...

First published in 2009. A catalogue record for this book is available from the British Library

ISBN: 978-1-844258-45-1

Published by Haynes Publishing, Sparkford, Yeovil, Somerset BA22 7JJ, UK
Tel: 01963 442030 Fax: 01963 440001 Int. tel: +44 1963 442030 Int. fax: +44 1963 440001
E-mail: sales@haynes.co.uk Website: www.haynes.co.uk

Haynes North America Inc., 861 Lawrence Drive, Newbury Park, California 91320, USA

Packaged for Haynes by Green Umbrella Publishing

Printed and bound by J F Print Ltd., Sparkford. Somerset

Special thanks to Fergus McKenna

MANAGEMENT Boll**ks

How to talk your way to the top...

Richard Havers

Brain Dump...

Just who is picking the low hanging fruit? Is brainstorming a thing of the past or do we now just do 'thought showers'? If you have ever spent time in a meeting contemplating yet another 'paradigm shift' then you will be the first to realize that at the end of the day it is all a load of. . .

For some people Genghis Khan was the earliest example of an extremely competent manager; although it's doubtful whether he ever wasted time on management speak – for him actions spoke louder than words. Management speak seems to have been gifted to the world by America. Chester Irving Edwards' 1938 book *Functions of the Executive* has a lot to answer for. With statements like, "The line of communication should not be interrupted when the organization is functioning," you could have guessed that it was only going to get worse.

Initially it was those on the cutting edge that talked the talk, soon middle, junior and even non-managers embraced this language as a means of getting ahead. Management speak is very seductive – the bottom line is we're all trying to leverage our fair share of the intellectual capital. Even politicians, who look increasingly like middle managers in marketing departments, have hi-jacked management speak to 'present', or at least try to differentiate, their ever more similar ideas from those of the other parties. It is now so pervasive that everyone in society at least grasps the basics of the language.

It's no different from the language as a whole; it's evolving year by year as new words get added to the lexicon almost every week. It would be wonderful to know who dreams some of it up. Who was the first numpty that uttered the immortal phrase, 'transferable skill set'? Who said 'impactfulness' and kept a straight face? Who decided it was a good idea to have hymn sheets in the office? But whatever the answer, who needs to walk the walk, when you can talk the talk?

While euphemisms have crept into management speak for just about every kind of business activity, recently one old fashioned piece of straight talk has come back into fashion. 'You're fired!' Still, it's better than if Geng his Khan had been your manager, in his case it would have been 'You're dead!'

Risk Aware

So how do you like our new non-gender specific working environment?

There'll be no more brainstorms at boardroom lunches! From now on it'll be idea showers. . . so much better for the digestion

Bianca, thank you for bringing those ideas to the table

Jason is our new product evangelist

We're introducing holistic solutions that demonstrate the company's cradle to grave management style

Maybe we could touch base on that when you're offline

I thought when he said to target the low hanging fruit it would be easy

Let's look under the bonnet shall we?

At Pure Ice Cream none of our strategic thinking is vanilla
CREAM
FIRE CURT
OVERHAUL
BY
FRANK BURK
BORO.
EPAIRED
PURE ICE
CREAM.

Have you got any more 360 ideas?

We need to get our ducks in a row

MANAGER

My door is
always open

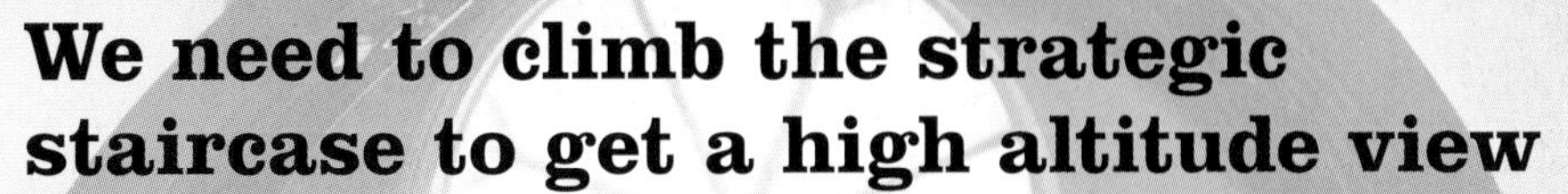

We need to climb the strategic staircase to get a high altitude view

Our fact based management strategy will empower us to implement a policy of best practice

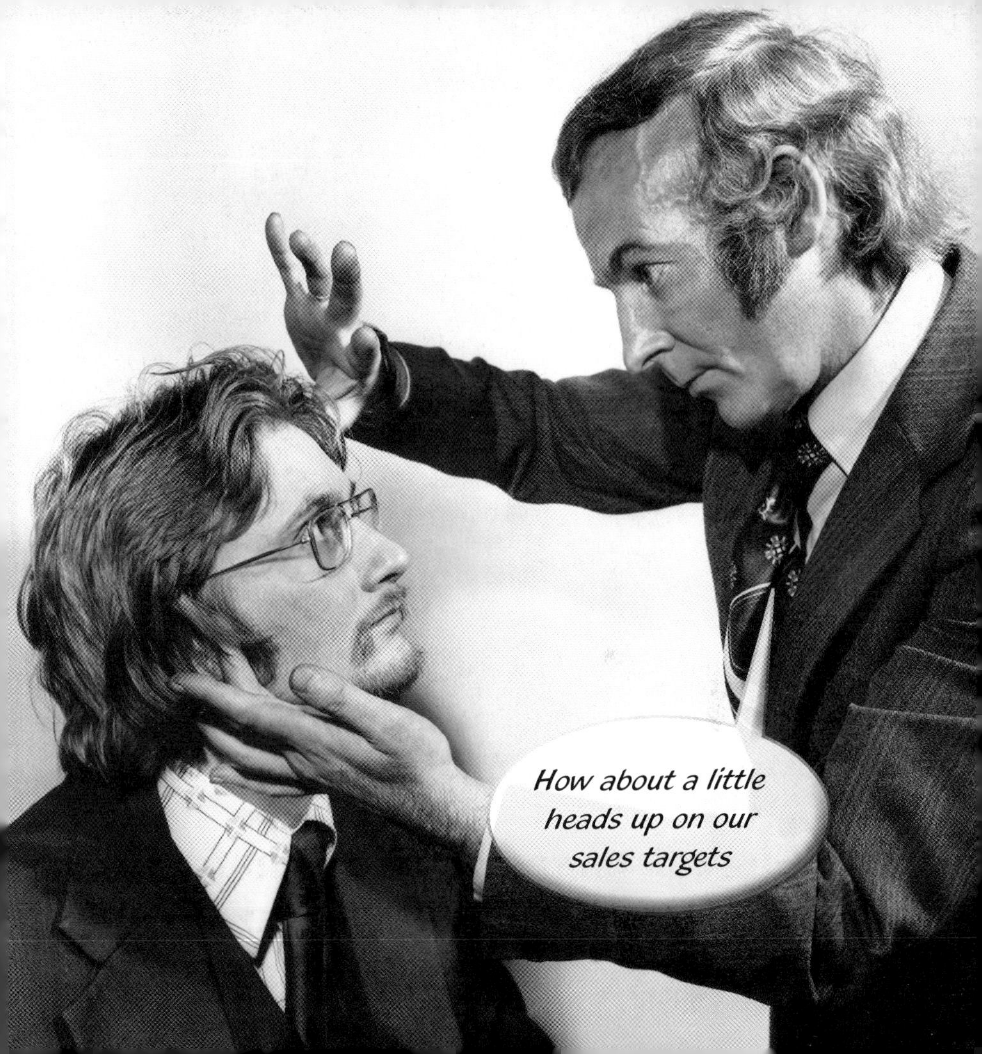
How about a little heads up on our sales targets

We need to stop thinking short term

We need a 24/7 approach to our day to day thinking

You need to step up to the plate on this and face the music

We need to orchestrate our response into a chorus of faith-based intelligence

Cheryl, I want you to be part of our ambitious change agenda

The paperless office concept needs a little work

The Daily Herald

I'm here to hone your leadership skills through mentoring

We need to do a great deal more to harness our corporate intellectual capital so as we don't under sell ourselves

I'm so sorry but that one just slipped off my radar

Two heads are better than one when it comes to problem solving

The sales team is being refocused to deliver on our core values

The simple ideas are the ones that hunt

It's our entity's away day; we're focusing on team building

Our sales manager is all fired up and pushing the envelope

At the end of the day the bottom line is. . .

It's important that we keep our customer pipeline aligned at all times

So we'll suck it and see

We're going to take a bath if
this b/s goes on much longer

Not another knee
jerk reaction

We'll have the marketing department jumping through a few more hoops

A 94.7% increase in our sales targets, we'll never do it

That's not quite what I had in mind when I said we need to address it through a focus group

*Moderately qualified, non-threatening straight male employee who gets ahead because he's a nice guy

Dress Down Friday

We are developing Chantelle's transferable skill set

We need to think big!

The sales team needs to get out there and press the flesh

Let's run that up the flagpole and see who salutes it

It would be so much more helpful if you addressed me in non-gender specific language

Crystal, the company is constantly vigilant in fighting the war on staff stress

Here at Clowns in Clover it's our staff that makes sure that if we didn't run a better business, we wouldn't have a better business to run

"CLOWNS
IN
CLOVER"

Natalia the company is committed to creating a working environment that promotes mutual respect

Tammi, I'm here to give you sensitive counseling while informing you of feedback results from your staff appraisal

I am not a 'human
resource', I am a person!

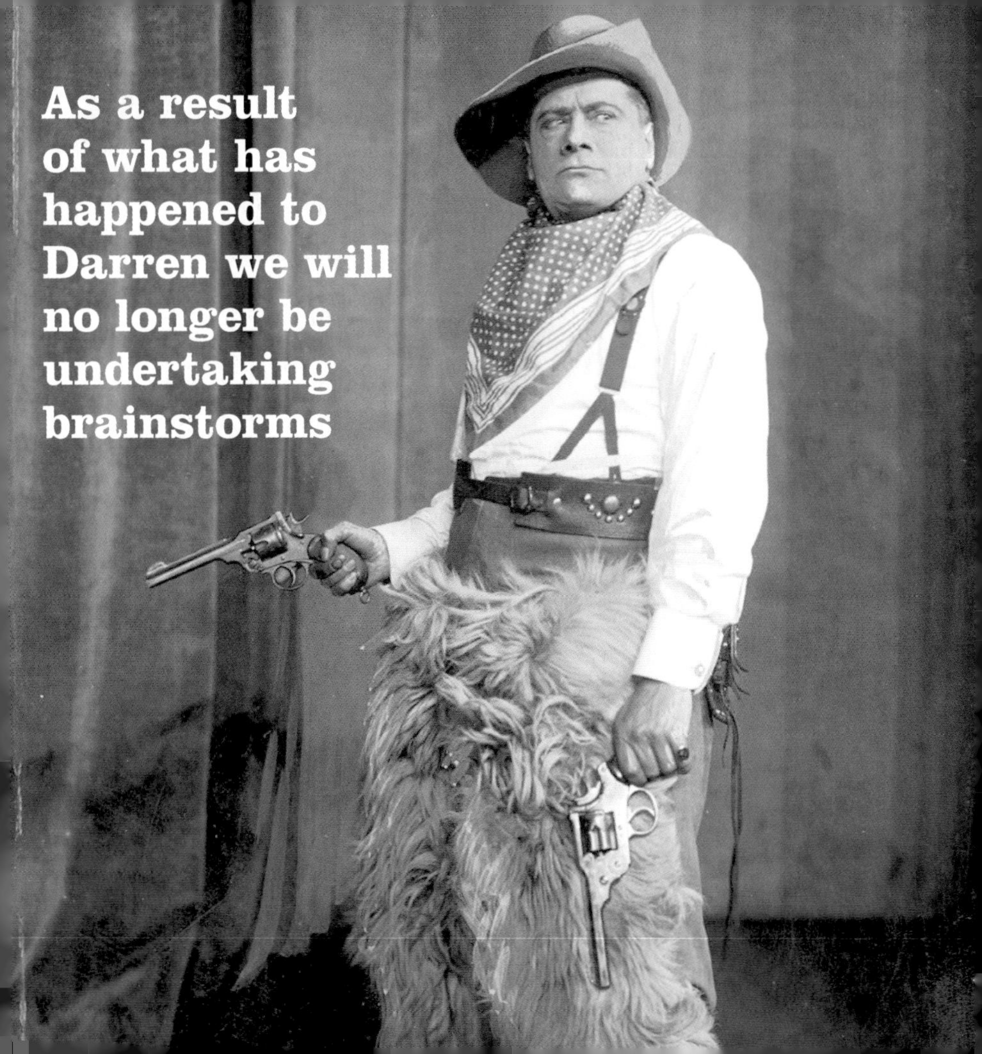
As a result
of what has
happened to
Darren we will
no longer be
undertaking
brainstorms

Sensitivity training

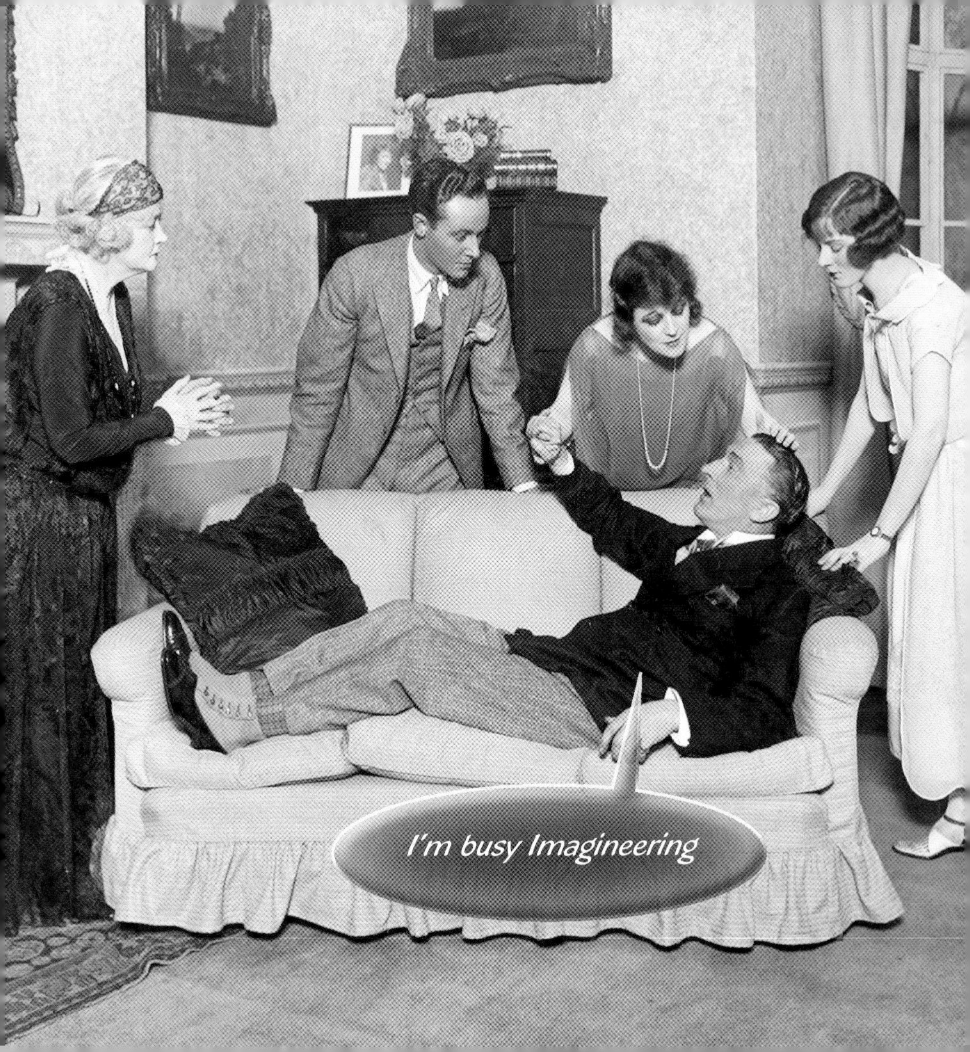
I'm busy Imagineering

Our concept of Matrix management is only to have direct line reporting

Let's benchmark our blue-sky thinking?

We must engage more fully with our stakeholders

We need a new cross media data related sales initiative to stimulate the market

It's time to take this company stratospheric

It's time we started singing off
the same hymn sheet

Comments such as 'you can't teach an old dog new tricks', or 'not old enough to command respect' are ageist, discriminatory, unlawful, and will create a liability for the originator and the employer

I think we need to keep going forward in order to achieve a win-win, while not losing sight of our exit strategy

We need to customize our thinking to be proactive to market demands

I'll let you know when I can open a communication dialogue with you on that

. . . and in closing could I add that there's a need to vertically integrate our zero based workflow parameters

Our company ethos is to provide a great work environment while treating each other with respect and dignity

I think he's the greatest corporate strategist I've ever met

We need more eyeballs
J
E
R

I C H O

We need a reality-based strategy that delivers results in real time without the need to double dip

We need to manage our deliverables

Let's try a little mindshare, shall we?

Modern integrated computerized HR/ training management systems can offer increased and sophisticated functionality

Chantelle, they can stuff their age diversity awareness programme

. . .and furthermore we must globalize the positioning of our world-class product

Jordan, I know our interactive management style has eradicated the need for meetings, but that won't stop us

Let's draw a line in the sand and then extrapolate it into the future, shall we?

It's head office on the phone Ricky; they're saying we need to dynamically reallocate resources to maximize our intellectual infrastructure

Our business plan has impactfulness written all over it and at the same time it's future proof

Good, I see you've all read the corporate identity manual

Dwayne,
we need to bolt on a more
robust skills matrix

We're going to take a
helicopter view of things

So, you think you could pick that up and run with it?
Yes, Darren, I'll knife and fork it

You can put bells and whistles on it but it's still déjà poo to me

To be honest Chantelle you really have managed to get your head around viral marketing so much better than the others

I'm a social entrepreneur with a
passion for web-enabled e-commerce
green marketing initiatives

We're a people business and we hit the ground running

We need to take that to the next level of granularity

We take a big picture view of
our human capital

Anybody would think there was an elephant in the room!

If you have to swallow a frog, don't look at it too long

It's not rocket science Darren; we have to constantly think outside the box

We seek passionate banking representatives to uphold our brand values

Let's have the CEO talk to the CFO so we can COCA*
*Cover our collective arses

Unless you meta-prioritize that data-dump, I'm going into meltdown

We'll touch base on our forward-looking statements

We're an industry leader
in value added bandwidth

Confucius he say... it's all a load of bollocks so not to worry